Contents

KW-223-168

Introduction

In the business of writing training, we live or die by the clarity with which we express ourselves. Every time we produce a document for a client, whether as part of the training itself or during pre- or post-course communication, that document remains as our 'voice'. It is what our clients judge us by. So it is vital that we are as clear in our thinking and writing as we urge others to be.

This guide is designed to help us achieve this: to produce Emphasis documents that are consistent and consistently excellent. It is primarily a resource, with tips on style and advice on usage, restricting its 'rules' to specific points of punctuation and grammar. And it stands as a work in progress, evolving as we encounter new queries and debate new points of style.

The most valuable of all talents is that of never using two words when one will do.

1

Tips for clear writing

Know your reader

We are all prone to becoming trapped in our own little world of 'getting the document done'. Yet writing that does not consider the reader is unlikely to succeed in its objectives, or perhaps even to be read at all. To ensure you get your message across, ask yourself why you are writing, what you are trying to say and to whom you are saying it. Make sure you are clear about what action you want your readers to take once they've read the document. In this way, you will tell them what they need to know, not what you've found out.

Know what you want to say

You need to put your important messages at the start, so make sure you know what they are before you begin writing. Test them out loud before you commit them to paper: if you can't make sense of them, how will your readers?

We waste a lot of time crafting sentences only to cut them (or have them cut) at the final edit. So it makes sense to sort out your thinking at the planning, not the writing, stage. Marshal your material in a way that is logical and transparent to your reader. And use subheads to show readers at a glance how your themes develop.

Reader-centred writing

Ask yourself:

1 Why am I writing this?

2 Who is it for?

3 What am I trying to say?

How to say what you mean

It *is* what you say, not the way that you say it (and that's what gets results). In business, good writing is invisible. You have failed if you force your reader to concentrate on the words rather than the message. There are specific ways in which you can hone your writing style to highlight what you are saying rather than how you say it.

The central readability principles are:

- **be direct**
- **use the active voice**
- **keep it short and simple (KISS)**
- **stick to one sentence, one idea**
- **proof it.**

The following pages examine each of these principles in turn, and give before and after examples showing the pitfalls in context.

Be direct

Be direct by addressing your readers as 'you' and referring to yourself, the writer, as 'we' or 'I' wherever possible. For example, in place of: 'The writers of this sentence advise readers to adopt this technique', write: 'We advise you to adopt this technique'. This will make your writing – and its relevance – easier to understand. 'You' and especially 'we' also make writing more confident, more transparent and more personal.

Make sure, too, that you write about what concerns your readers rather than about your organisation's internal processes.

Before

Delegates are instructed to send in examples of their writing before training courses. The office manager receives the samples and sends them to the trainers, who analyse them to get a better idea of where delegates' strengths and weaknesses lie.

After

Please send us an example of your writing before the course. We will analyse it so we can give you an idea of where your strengths and weaknesses lie.

Use the active voice

Using the active voice more is the single biggest thing that will give your writing a bit of oomph. If a piece of writing seems unspeakably dull, it's probably because the writer has overused the passive voice.

Consider this sentence:
Allowances were made by the trainer for late arrivals.

This sentence is in the passive voice. The person or thing doing the action ('the trainer') follows the action ('were made').

The active voice puts the 'doer' – in grammar terms, the *agent* – first. This makes the sense clearer and the wording less clumsy:
The trainer made allowances for late arrivals.
Or
The trainer allowed for late arrivals.

You could also write the passive sentence like this:
Allowances were made for late arrivals.

This sentence does not tell you who took the action it describes (there is no agent). This is because, unlike the active voice, the passive allows you to remove the agent. So if a sentence leaves you asking: 'By whom?', it's passive. This is why the passive produces very opaque text. Using the active voice forces you to be more specific and, again, more confident.

Before	**After** 	**Or**
It was assumed by management that the changes to working practices had been implemented.	Managers assumed that staff had implemented the changes to working practices.	Managers assumed staff had changed their working practices.

Keep it short and simple (KISS)

Make sure you write what you mean by saying it aloud. As far as possible, use everyday language – the kind of language you use when you talk – to get your message across to your reader.

Be rigorous in your editing. Are you using the best word for the job? What do you mean? Is there a simpler way to say it? When you think you've finished, try cutting the content by a third.

Using jargon is fine for an internal or expert readership, provided you are certain they'll understand it. But avoid it when writing for external or non-expert readers. Keep abbreviations and acronyms to a minimum. And explain them when they do crop up.

Use verbs (which express actions) rather than nouns (which refer to things, people and places): it's the verbs that make language dynamic. Be especially vigilant for those heavy nouns ending in -tion or -sion, eg recommendation: this *nominalisation* (creating a noun from the verb) can make your writing clunky and boring to read, as it attracts redundant words. (This is why we call these words 'waffle magnets' at Emphasis.) See the table opposite for some examples.

And use concrete terms rather than abstract (or meaningless) generalities: 'Help with giving up smoking' rather than 'Strategies for smoking cessation' (the title of a leaflet we found in a local pharmacy).

	Verb		Nominalisation
Use	implement/do	not	undertake the implementation of
	consider/think about	not	give consideration to
	complete	not	achieve completion of
	decide	not	reach a decision
	recommend	not	make a recommendation to

Before

The aim of this document is to provide an outline of systemic operations to facilitate the implementation of methodology that will assist the team in the avoidance of inconsistency in the wording used in training materials.

After

This document outlines how we can be consistent with the wording we use in training materials.

Use the *Jargon buster* on page 28 to make sure you don't slip into management-speak or woolly wording.

One sentence, one idea

Keep your sentences short. Your reader will find it easier to understand what you are saying if you stick to one idea per sentence. If you write a long sentence, with many asides and qualifying clauses (like this one), your reader will find it hard to catch and then follow your drift and will probably have to return to the beginning of the sentence in order to make sense of it and in turn – and perhaps most importantly – act on it.

Aim for an average of 17 words per sentence; a maximum of 35. But varying your rhythm is key: try inserting the odd two- or three-word sentence for impact. It's easy. And it may well keep your reader awake.

Before

Whilst the organisation currently relies on sponsorship from small enterprises and individuals, the cooperation of large corporate bodies, without whose funding we will not be able to provide the services our clients require, is now essential if we are to campaign successfully for legislative changes that will improve the lives of many sectors of the population.

 ## After

We need funding to lobby for legislative changes that will improve people's lives. At the moment, we rely on sponsorship from small enterprises and individuals. But this is not enough. Financial support from large corporate bodies is now essential if we are to provide the services our clients require and campaign successfully for change.

Keep an eye on paragraph length, too. Try to stick to one main point per paragraph: if you can't sum up that point in a few words in the margin, you have probably tried to cram in too much information.

Proof it!

Proofreading isn't an optional extra: make time for it. Try to create some distance between writing the document and proofing it. Print it out and come back to it when you're fresh. And try to proofread away from your desk: this will help you read it as a reader, not as the writer. Use a ruler to guide you, and a pencil to point to each word individually. This will stop your brain reading what it expects to see rather than what's actually there.

Ten top tips for writing well

1. **Know your reader.**

2. **Know what you want to say.**

3. **Be direct.**

4. **Use the active voice.**

5. **Keep it short and simple (KISS).**

6. **Stick to one sentence, one idea.**

7. **Keep paragraphs short.**

8. **Use subheads that summarise the content.**

9. **Edit, then edit again.**

10. **Proofread on hard copy, and when you're fresh.**

I try to leave out the parts that people skip.

Elmore Leonard

2
Writing for the web

We behave differently online: we want a specific piece of information, and we want it now. Most visitors to a website will give it between five and ten seconds to prove its worth. We are also more likely to scan the text for key words, rather than read a page from beginning to end.

As a web writer, your challenge is to make it as easy as possible for readers to complete their particular tasks quickly and painlessly. This section outlines how you can use structure and language to achieve this. The principles for hard-copy writing all apply to writing for the web, but there are some variations.

First things first

There's a lot of information out there already. Do you have to write this page? Is the material already there on a different page on your site? Can you link to it to avoid duplicating effort?

Once you have considered these questions, work out how many pages you need to convey your information. Stick to one topic per page. And make sure each page is self-explanatory and self-contained. It should stand as an 'island' of information: your reader should be able to access it from anywhere and have it make sense.

Know your audience

Apply the same reader-centred approach as for hard-copy writing. If anything, be even more rigorous. Imagine who is likely to be visiting the site – what they like, what their attitudes are and what they're looking for – and keep these typical visitors in mind with everything you write for the web.

With such short attention spans, your readers need to see that you are giving them what they are looking for right up at the top of the page. Use meaningful titles, eg 'Why we're different' and 'How to book a course'. And make sure you get your main message across in the first couple of lines.

Subheads and formatting

Use regular, clear subheads to break up the text and make it easy for your reader to jump to the appropriate section. Make your subheads explicit, rather than using bland, general wording. So '40 years in the business' is better than 'Our experience'. Combined, your subheads should tell the story.

Avoid using bold for key words in the body text, but make sure you include key words in your subheads, eg 'Programmes tailored to your needs' and 'Detailed writing analysis'.

Keep underline for hyperlinks (see *Hyperlinks*, page 18):
   Pre-course <u>writing analysis</u> identifies the areas you need to work on.

Avoid using italics: words in italics are difficult to read on screen.

Hyperlinks

Each time you link to another site, you make it more likely that visitors will leave yours, never to return. So use hyperlinks to other sites sparingly.

Ensuring that links to other sites open in another window will help stop visitors from losing their thread. But linking within your own site too much is also distracting. Try to group hyperlinks at the bottom of a page, if possible, as well as placing them in the body text.

Make sure too that you have content on every page: relegating everything to a hyperlink is both irritating and time-consuming for the reader. Never put a full stop after a hyperlink, even at the end of a sentence.

Paragraphs

Keep paragraphs short. Use subheads (see page 17) to signpost content more often than you would in hard-copy documents. And don't try to fit too much onto a page. If you find your page extends way beyond a screen's worth, think again about how you have organised your material. You can probably break it down into more digestible chunks.

Get to the point

Keep up to date

Don't mess around with background and waffly welcomes. Get rid of any 'We have written this page to help you…' stuff. Use the readability techniques in this guide to write concise, unambiguous text. Pay special attention to sentence length: if in doubt, put that full stop in.

Review your pages regularly, making sure any dates, eg course dates, are updated. Out-of-date information will undermine the content of your whole site.

Web writing that doesn't work

This extract is from the building standards page of a (fictitious) local council website.

Before

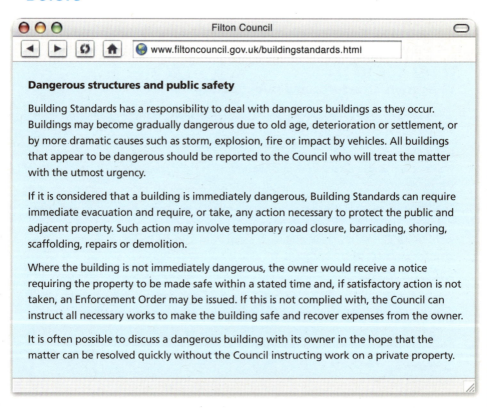

Filton Council

www.filtoncouncil.gov.uk/buildingstandards.html

Dangerous structures and public safety

Building Standards has a responsibility to deal with dangerous buildings as they occur. Buildings may become gradually dangerous due to old age, deterioration or settlement, or by more dramatic causes such as storm, explosion, fire or impact by vehicles. All buildings that appear to be dangerous should be reported to the Council who will treat the matter with the utmost urgency.

If it is considered that a building is immediately dangerous, Building Standards can require immediate evacuation and require, or take, any action necessary to protect the public and adjacent property. Such action may involve temporary road closure, barricading, shoring, scaffolding, repairs or demolition.

Where the building is not immediately dangerous, the owner would receive a notice requiring the property to be made safe within a stated time and, if satisfactory action is not taken, an Enforcement Order may be issued. If this is not complied with, the Council can instruct all necessary works to make the building safe and recover expenses from the owner.

It is often possible to discuss a dangerous building with its owner in the hope that the matter can be resolved quickly without the Council instructing work on a private property.

This page hasn't been written with the reader in mind: there is unnecessary background detail and it doesn't make clear at the start what the main message is. Without subheads, it is also difficult to follow the logic. The language is not as direct (see *Be direct*, page 8) and active (see *Use the active voice*, page 9) as it could be. And there are no contact details, which undermines the practicality of the page as a whole. Here's a rewritten version that gets to the point, signposts the information clearly and tells readers all they need to know.

After

Dangerous structures and public safety

If you think a building is dangerous, please <u>report it to us</u> in the Building Standards team and we'll treat the matter with the utmost urgency.

Legal powers
We can often discuss a dangerous building with its owner and resolve the matter quickly. But we also have legal powers to take action to make buildings safe.

The action we take will depend on how dangerous the building is. If it's not immediately dangerous, we will send a notice to the owner, requiring them to make the property safe within a stated time. If the owner doesn't comply with initial requests, we may then issue an Enforcement Order.

Emergency measures
We will evacuate the building if we think it is immediately dangerous. We may also take other actions to protect the public. These may include temporarily closing the road, or barricading, shoring, scaffolding, repairing or even demolishing the building – recovering expenses from the owner where necessary.

Contact us
Contact us on 08457 654321 or email <u>buildingstandards@filton.gov.uk</u>

We're here to help you.

True eloquence consists of saying all that should be, not all that could be, said.

François de La Rochefoucauld

3
Writing email

Many of the 'rules' of email usage rely on common sense and are, to some extent, idiosyncratic: we all have our own favourite methods for structuring, prioritising and archiving messages. Here are a few tips for getting the most out of email – and ensuring your reader actually reads your messages.

Is anyone there?

Unbelievable as it may seem, not everyone checks their emails hourly or even daily. Don't fret over a lack of response until you have tangible cause to do so. If you need an urgent reply, try sending a short test message first to check that your recipient is actually there. Or, better still, pick up the phone.

Calm down

Email is unforgiving. Without facial expression and tone of voice, it's very easy to get it wrong. What you thought was a pithy, to-the-point message might come across as terse, bossy, or – worse – aggrieved.

Take your time responding to messages that anger or upset you. Remove the recipient's address before you write anything, so you don't send it prematurely. And save your reply as a draft to re-read later when you've calmed down.

That witty response may also, alas, fall flat. Successful humour on screen takes careful thought and knowledge of your recipient. If you don't have time for either of these, keep it straight. (See also *Print and proof*, page 27.)

Add attachments first

We've all done it: sent a message with attachments – without the attachments. Try adopting this routine for every message you send:

1. **Add the attachment(s).**

2. **Write the message.**

3. **Add the subject line.**

4. **Write the recipient's address.**

It's very simple, but it does work. Without an address, the message isn't going anywhere. And if you always add the attachments first, you'll be less likely to forget them. With 'Reply to' messages, try deleting the recipient's address before starting at number 1.

Use a meaningful subject line

Reel in your recipient with a relevant, unambiguous subject line. For example, 'Chapter 4 update?' will probably provoke a quicker response than 'Various'. Asking a question will often get a speedy reply, as the recipient feels they can give a brief answer before getting on with other more complex emails or tasks.

Remember to re-title a message that you have been batting to and fro, to make it relevant to the particular point in that message. For the same reason, give new subject lines to messages that have been forwarded endlessly and no longer have any relevance to the original title.

Be professional

Email has dispensed with much of the formality of traditional business writing. Using 'Hi' or just the recipient's first name then 'Kind regards' or 'Many thanks' keeps the tone direct and approachable. But beware of being too informal, especially across cultures or with recipients in a superior position. For a first contact, err on the side of caution, eg use 'Dear' rather than 'Hi'. You can always become less formal when you become more familiar with their preferred style.

Keep it snappy

Use the KISS principles (see *Keep it short and simple*, page 10) to keep the content concise. And try to restrict the body of the message to one screen. If you can't, use subheads or put the bulk of the information in an attachment, which you can then format in an easy-to-read way.

Print and proof

Always print and proofread important emails before you send them (see *Proof it!*, page 13). Not only will you then spot any embarrassing typos, but you will pick up on repetition and woolly phrasing when you see the message in black and white. If you want to use less paper, make a PDF of your email and proofread that onscreen – it's not as good as reading hard copy but it works better than re-reading the email itself. As with all writing, try to leave some time between the writing and the proofing of the message.

Try sending it to yourself as well. Oddly, reading a message in your own inbox puts you more in the frame of mind of the reader. This is a useful trick for monitoring your tone and spotting out-of-place remarks.

And don't SHOUT!

Avoid writing in upper case: it's IRRITATING and unnecessary.

Remove the recipient's address before writing a reply, so that you don't send it prematurely. See *Calm down*, page 24.

Here is a list of clichés, jargon and management-speak that we typically advise others to avoid using. We should practise what we preach.

add value to	**improve**
adjacent to	**next to**
as to	**about, on, of** (often redundant)
at an early date	**soon**
at this moment in time	**now** (often redundant)
bottom line	**most important thing, main point**
deliverables	(Avoid: say what they are, eg **Results**? **Reports**?)
going forward	(Usually redundant: rarely does life go backward.)
engage with	**talk to, contact**
in close proximity to	**near**
in the case of	**with**
in the field of	**in**
is able to	**can**
joined-up	**avoid**
leverage (vb)	**make the most of** (in non-financial context)
outside of	**outside**
on an ongoing basis	**regularly, periodically, continually**
on occasion	**sometimes**
prior to	**before**
step change	(Avoid. What is the change? What does it mean?)
with respect to	**about**
utilise	**use**

4

← Jargon buster

Simplicity is the ultimate sophistication.

Leonardo da Vinci

5

Writing for a global audience

There's more to writing for a non-British reader than making decisions about whether to use UK or US spelling. (We use UK: see *Problem words*, page 50, for more on spelling.) This section offers a few tips on how to write for a global audience without confusing or irritating your readers with unfamiliar words, concepts or references.

Avoid abbreviations and acronyms

Any collection of letters may have a different meaning in other countries. So while the BBC means the British Broadcasting Corporation to UK readers, it may also stand for the Bat-lovers of British Columbia. Or the Boy Buglers of Canberra.

Use abbreviations or acronyms sparingly with a global audience and always explain them in full the first time you use them.

Be careful with colloquial expressions and popular culture

Don't make assumptions about your reader's familiarity with a particular country's culture. Many readers will have no idea what to do if you ask them to keep their eye on the ball, give you the nod or push the envelope. Nor might they be familiar with being in the black, piggy banks, ivory towers or sacred cows. Avoid such expressions.

Explain local business terms

Explain terms such as redundancy ('retrenchment' in South Africa), downsizing or brainstorming. Or avoid them altogether.

Don't talk about the weather!

Avoid talking about seasons at all, never mind whether they're particularly hot, cold or wet. Your summer is someone else's winter. And 'the cold winter of 2010' will mean very little to most of the globe. Refer to specific months instead.

Use simple language

Always go for the clearest option when choosing which words to use. Avoid phrasal verbs, eg turn up. So ask if she came to the meeting, not if she turned up. And apply the KISS principles (see *Keep it short and simple*, page 10), using concrete terms rather than waffly abstracts.

Before
We need to think outside the box on this one and come up with transitional operating procedures so that we can put this project to bed asap.

After
We need to be more efficient so we can finish the project by Friday.

The chief virtue that language can have is clarity.

Hippocrates

6

Emphasis house style

A. Layout

Fonts

We use two different fonts, one for course manuals and one for client documents. All manuals use variations of Frutiger for body text, box text and subheads.

For client documents, click the Office logo (top left corner) in Microsoft Word, then New, then select the Emphasis template. All margins and line spaces are set in the template, so there is no need to press return twice for paragraph breaks. Instead, highlight the text and select the right style.

Heading 1 / Heading 1

Heading 2 / Heading 2 / Heading 2

Crosshead

Subhead

Body text

For reference, here are the styles:

Heading 1:	ITC Avant Garde, 22pt, red or grey
Heading 2:	ITC Avant Garde, 16pt, black, red or grey
Crosshead:	ITC Avant Garde, 12pt, red
Subhead:	ITC Avant Garde, 10.5pt, red
Body text:	Arial 10pt

Note that all headings and subheads are sentence case, ie no capitals apart from the initial one.

Bullets

In our Word documents, we use square body bullets. The template sets the line spaces before and after, so you don't need to add them. Bullets should have at least one introductory sentence; never put a bulleted list straight after a subhead.

Introduce bullets with a colon. Use:
❑ lower case
❑ no punctuation
❑ a full stop after the last bullet if it ends the sentence (as this one does).

Bullets (and sub-bullets) that are whole sentences should begin with a capital letter and each should end with a full stop, as shown below:

❑ Be consistent with bullet structure.
  ▪ Do not mix whole sentences and fragments in one list.
  ▪ Indent sub-bullets under the main bullet.
  ▪ Sub-bullets are smaller and black.

Tables

Table format is also set in the template, and looks like this:

Table header	Table header
Table text • Table bullet • Table bullet • Table bullet More table text etc.	Table text • Table bullet • Table bullet • Table bullet More table text etc.

Caption style: make sure each figure/table has a caption like this.

Extracts

Indent quotes or extracts of more than 50 words. Do not use italics in this case, as it makes them hard to read. Introduce them with a colon (see *Colons*, page 44).

Bold and underline

Use bold for headings and subheads. Avoid using bold to highlight words within text.

Use underline for hyperlinks only, not for headings or to emphasise a word.

Italics

Use italics for:

- books, publications, newspapers and radio and television programmes, eg *Troublesome Words* by Bill Bryson, *The Times*
- foreign phrases that are not assimilated into English, including Latin terms, but use the English alternative whenever possible
- emphasis in text, but use sparingly and try to find an alternative expression if possible: 'style *does* matter' or 'but style matters'
- cross references.

Do not use italics for brand names, except where the brand name is also a publication, eg Write Here (the business writing forum) but *The Write Stuff* (a publication).

B. Names and numbers

Company name

Our company name is Emphasis Training Ltd. Use the full name in legal/contract documents only. For general client documents, refer to the company as Emphasis:

❏ Emphasis trainers are the best in the business.

Note that the use of lower case for company name and description is normally restricted to our logo.

Capitals

Avoid unnecessary capitals, but stick to the rules below:

Job and course titles

Use lower case unless it is a formal title or a brand name:

❏ The trainers are busy.
❏ Rob Ashton, Chief Executive of Emphasis Training Ltd, has arrived.
❏ Emphasis style guide, *The Write Stuff*, and writing forum, Write Here
❏ UK Prime Minister David Cameron
❏ David Cameron, the UK's Conservative prime minister
❏ A number of prime ministers attended.

Likewise, governments are lower case unless you are referring to a particular administration:

❏ The Government announced the abolition of the 10p tax band.
❏ Representatives from governments across Europe were united.

Courses should have an initial capital only:

❏ Our courses include: High-impact writing, Writing for the web and Creating persuasive proposals.

Regions

Countries, states and regions regarded as having a distinct identity need capitals: France, Northern Ireland, West Virginia, the South East.

Areas that do not have a distinct identity do not need capitals: the south of Norway, western France.

Addresses

Use open punctuation – do not punctuate addresses:

> Mr R Smith
> Emphasis Training Ltd
> 130 Queen's Road
> Brighton
> BN1 3WB

Likewise, do not put a comma after salutations and valedictions:

> Dear Mr Smith
> Dear Fiona
> Yours sincerely
> Kind regards

Writing numbers

Write out numbers one to ten in words.
Use figures for 11 and above: 11; 61; 11,000.
Avoid mixing words and figures in the same phrase:

❑   You can order in multiples of 9, 12 or 16 (not 'nine, 12 or 16').

Always use figures if decimals or fractions are involved: 6.25 or 6¼.
Write ordinals (first, second, third etc) in full (not 1st, 2nd, 3rd).
Write fractions below one in full and hyphenate them: two-thirds of the class.

Thousands, millions and billions

Write thousands as 60,000 (not 60K).
Use a comma for four digits or more (but not in dates): 5,000, 5000BC.

Write millions as 60 million or 60m (not 60,000,000).

File sizes should always be written as abbreviations: 45Kb;1.8Mb.
A billion is a thousand million (1,000,000,000), not a million million.
Write billions as 6 billion or 6bn (not 6,000,000,000).

Percentages

Use per cent in running text (as opposed to tables etc), not the % sign:

❑   A good 95 per cent of delegates leave satisfied.
❑   Almost all delegates (95 per cent) leave satisfied.

Date, time and range

Write dates in this format: 7 September 2009.
❑   The meeting is on 8 March 2010.

Use these forms rather than the 24-hour clock: 9.30am, 12 noon, 5pm.

Use twentieth century, not 20th century.

Use from/to, between/and or X–X. But don't mix and match:
❑   from 9am to 5pm
❑   between 9am and 5am
❑   course time: 9am–5pm.

(Note that the dash is an en-rule, not a hyphen: see page 46 for
more on dashes.)

If spanning dates in the same century, drop the first two digits of the
second date: 1967–69.

But keep them if the dates span different centuries: 1999–2008.

Do not use apostrophes for collective dates: 1990s (not 1990's).

C. Punctuation

Abbreviations and acronyms

Do not use full stops in abbreviations or acronyms (abbreviations that can be pronounced as words). For example:

❏ ie, eg, etc, am, pm, ltd, UK, US, Dr, Mrs, m, kg, km, UNESCO

Precede 'eg' and 'ie' with a comma, eg as in this example, or with a bracket (eg as shown here). Do not use a comma or colon after 'eg' or 'ie':

❏ To find out more, enrol on one of our courses, eg High-impact writing.

Do not use apostrophes to make abbreviations plural: HGVs, CVs.

Write acronyms that are made up of parts of words, not just initial letters, with initial capitals only:

❏ Ofcom – Office of Communications

The first time you use an abbreviated term, write it out in full followed by the abbreviation or acronym in brackets. This is not necessary if the abbreviation is so familiar to your audience that it is the more often used and more readily understood form, eg HIV, DNA, MP.

Ampersands (&)

Avoid using an ampersand (&) unless it forms part of a company name:

❏ Ernst & Young, Marks & Spencer

Do not use it as a general substitute for 'and'.

Apostrophes

Use apostrophes to:

☐ represent missing letters, eg don't, isn't, Helen's early
☐ denote periods of time, eg a day's leave, a week's holiday, in three weeks' time
☐ show possession, eg Jane's bag, the group's project, workers' rights.

For nouns ending in 's', follow these guidelines:

☐ singular: use the normal 's, eg his boss's car, the business's success
☐ singular proper nouns: go by sound – in general, use 's for monosyllabic names and ' alone for polysyllabic names, eg James's book, Cass's sister, Emphasis' trainers, Dickens' novels, in Jesus' name (note that biblical and classical names usually take ' alone)
☐ plural: use ', eg the Joneses' dog, other businesses' problems
☐ singular in meaning, but plural in form: use ', eg the United States' foreign policy, the Philippines' president.

For joint possession, eg Janet and John's book, use an apostrophe only after the second name. Use an apostrophe after each name, eg David's and Sarah's books, for separate possession, ie each person owns different book(s):

☐ Bill and Nancy's address (they live together)
☐ Bill's and Nancy's addresses (they live apart).

Do not use an apostrophe where 'its' is a possessive pronoun, eg the dog ate its bone. It's is always short for 'it is' or 'it has'. In general, do not use an apostrophe to make a plural, including in dates and abbreviations, eg peas, HGVs, CVs, 1990s. Exceptions arise only where to omit the apostrophe might cause ambiguity, eg the do's and don'ts, A's and B's.

Brackets

Use round brackets to:

- include optional information, eg almost half (48 per cent)

- explain a term or introduce an abbreviation, eg Many people use upper case (capital letters) for writing headings. Send me the summary review memorandum (SRM)

- cross-refer, eg Be careful with square brackets (see below). Refer to the plain English dictionary (page 43).

Use square brackets to:

- include an editorial comment or direction, eg Staff will receive a huge bonus [Rob, please confirm]

- include a clarification that is not part of quoted text, eg The position [in business writing training] is far from clear.

The full stop should lie inside the closing bracket if the whole sentence is bracketed, and outside if the bracketed section forms only part of the whole sentence, eg Hope this helps. (Look at the website too.) If you'd like more help, get in touch (or look at the website).

Colons

Use colons to:

- introduce lists, eg There are three things we need: time, investment and creativity

- introduce bullets

- introduce long quotes, which will also be indented (see *Extracts*, page 38). Introduce short quotes with a comma (see *Commas*, opposite).

- emphasise a question, eg The question is: are their traditional business processes up to the job?
- lead the reader from an idea (usually in the form of a statement that could be a complete sentence) to its consequence or logical continuation, eg He was very tired when he did that piece of work: there were lots of mistakes in it.

Compare this final use of the colon, where there is a step forward in argument (often cause: effect, or fact: explanation), with the similar use of the semicolon, which links balanced or parallel clauses (see *Semicolons*, page 49). Use lower case after a colon, except when introducing a list of bullets that are whole sentences (see *Bullets*, page 37).

Commas

Use commas to:

- help the reader understand the sense of something, eg However, you might feel the new law will make a difference. However you might feel, the new law will make a difference.
- denote a natural pause, often after a secondary clause at the beginning of a sentence, eg Unfortunately, this is not true. Although it was raining, we decided to go for a picnic.
- show that information is extra to the main idea, eg The photocopier, which is on the second floor, needs repairing.
- separate items in a list, eg She wanted eggs, ham and bacon.
- denote how items are split in lists, eg The sandwiches they stocked were ham, chicken, ham and tomato, and chicken and cucumber.
- introduce short quotes, eg Clara says, 'We need to act quickly.'

Dashes

Use dashes to:

- explain, paraphrase or draw a conclusion from something you have just written, eg He had a natural flair for leadership – hence his promotion.

- highlight a parenthetical point, eg The show – a runaway success – has just had its final week.

- show a range or sequence, eg 1999–2004, A–Z, 5pm–6pm, London–Edinburgh line.

There are two kinds of dash: the em-rule (—) and the en-rule (–). British style typically uses the en-rule; American style, the em-rule. At Emphasis, we use the en-rule. For the first two bullets above, be sure to put a space either side of it. (American em-rules don't use spaces.)

Do not confuse an en-rule with a hyphen: it is twice the length (see *Hyphens*, opposite).

Exclamation marks

Use exclamation marks sparingly and singly to express surprise, shock or despair, eg I don't believe it!

Do not use them to add excitement to dull writing. It doesn't work.

Full stops

Use plenty. And put a single space after a full stop.

Hyphens

Use hyphens to:

- join words in adjectival phrases before the noun, ie where the words work together to describe something, eg long-term solution, fault-finding technique, an information-led society. Do not use a hyphen if the first word ends in -ly, eg highly acclaimed novel.

- form some compound words. For Emphasis documents, follow the guidelines below. Refer to the *Collins English Dictionary* if the word you need isn't listed. If it's not listed there, split it.

One word:	Hyphenated:	Separate words:
breakdown (n)	cost-effective	break down (v)
changeover (n)	decision-maker	per cent
cooperate	eye-opener	version that is up to date
coordinate	full-time	web page
database	high-impact writing	
email	in-house courses	
inbox	like-minded	
laptop	self-assured	
online	up-to-date version	
percentage		
proactive		
proofread		
website		
worldwide		

Question marks

Use question marks:

❑   for direct questions, eg What are we going to do?

Do not use for sentences such as: I wonder if you could let me know.

Quotation marks

Use single quotation marks for direct speech and for highlighting words or phrases. Use double quotation marks only for a quote within a quote. Introduce short quotes with a comma (see *Commas*, page 45) and long quotes with a colon (see *Colons*, page 44).

Put the punctuation within the quotation marks only if it's part of the quote. Quoting a complete sentence means quoting the full stop too. So it goes inside the quotation marks. But quoting part of the sentence doesn't, so the full stop goes outside. The following passage illustrates most eventualities:

> She said, 'The food wasn't even hot.'
>
> She said that the food was far from the promised 'sizzlingly smashing'.
>
> She said, 'The food wasn't even hot and all the manager could say was, "Better eat it quickly then," which wasn't very helpful.'
>
> 'I will not be coming back,' she said.
>
> 'I will not be coming back,' she said, 'even if they beg me.'
>
> 'I will not,' she repeated, 'be coming back.'
>
> How many people said, 'We're not coming back'?
>
> She asked, 'Are you coming back?'
>
> Did she ask, 'Are you coming back?'
>
> 'All I can say,' she said, 'is that if they don't apologise …'

Semicolons

Think of semicolons as 'super commas'. Use them to:

- separate long phrases in a list when at least one of the phrases contains a comma, eg You will need the following items: climbing boots (or strong walking shoes); two pairs of lightweight trousers; and – most importantly – a waterproof jacket, which must have zipped internal pockets.

- link two related clauses that could otherwise be joined with 'and' or 'but', eg Some people do their best work in the morning; others are at their best in the afternoon.

D. Problem words

This section deals with words that are commonly mis-used, mis-spelt or otherwise abused. If you can't find what you're looking for anywhere else in this guide, look here.

affect/effect

Both are commonly used as verbs but mean different things. To affect means 'to influence' or 'to adopt a pose, assume the manner of' (as in 'affectation'):

❑   This weather affected my mood; he affected indifference.

To effect means 'to bring about' or 'accomplish':

❑   The council effected a change to the rubbish collection rota.

Only 'effect' is commonly used as a noun ('affect' as a noun relates to emotional state and is used only in a narrow psychological context):

❑   The effects of the hurricane were felt across the island.

among/amongst

Use 'among'.

anyone/any one

One word when referring to a person, eg Is anyone there? Otherwise, two words, eg He received three job offers, any one of which would have suited him.

centre on/around

Use 'centre on' and 'revolve around'.

compare to/with

Use 'compare to' to liken things, eg Shall I compare thee to a summer's day?; He compared Jenny to her mum. (He felt Jenny to be similar to her mum.)

Use 'compare with' to consider similarities or differences, eg He compared Jenny with her mum. (He assessed the two women's relative merits.)

complement/ compliment

The first means 'to support, make whole or expand', eg This project complements the work we did last year. The second means 'to encourage or praise', eg He paid a compliment to Jenny. Likewise, complementary therapy supports or broadens existing treatment; complimentary treatment is free.

comprise

No 'of' with comprise, eg The group comprises a trainer, an accountant and a salesperson.

Or try 'consists of' instead, eg The group consists of a trainer, an accountant and a salesperson.

continual/continuous

A continual buzzing is a noise that happens repeatedly but not constantly. Continuous buzzing doesn't stop.

data

Treat 'data' as singular, eg Send me this data (not these data). Technically data is plural, as is agenda. But nobody uses the singular 'agendum', and the singular 'datum' likewise comes across as pedantic.

dependant/ dependent

Your dependants are the ones who depend on you, such as your family. Dependent means 'contingent upon', eg The contract renewal is dependent on your performance.

disinterested/ uninterested

If you are disinterested in something, you are impartial and have no stake in the outcome. If you are uninterested, you simply couldn't care less.

fewer/less

Use 'fewer' for countable things and 'less' for uncountable things, eg There are fewer bottles but less milk.

Sometimes the boundaries are blurred, eg It is less than ten miles to London. Here, the ten miles is thought of as one total distance, rather than ten units of one mile. Apply common sense if in doubt.

focusing/focussing

Both are correct. Use the version with one 's'.

'h' at the beginning of a word

Use 'an' before a word beginning with a silent 'h', eg 'an hour' but 'a hostage' and 'a hotel'.

however

Punctuation around 'however' depends on how you use it. Where it is an aside, put commas around it. However, if it starts a new point (as it does here), it must follow a full stop or semicolon and not a comma. Consider these examples:

- These things, however, are bound to happen.
- These things are bound to happen; however, we must find a solution.
- However, these things are bound to happen.
- However these things happen, we must find a solution.

-ise/-ize

Use the standard British convention of -ise where there is a choice, eg realise, organise, apologise.

lead/led

The regular past and past participle of 'to lead' is 'led', not 'lead'. 'Lead' (as a noun) is what you used to find in a pencil or a piece of piping.

momentarily

In UK English, this means 'for a moment', eg I momentarily lost my bearings. In US English, momentarily commonly means 'at any moment', eg I'll finish this momentarily. Stick to the UK version.

practice/practise

In UK English, 'practice' is the noun, 'practise' the verb, eg I need to do my piano practice, but I also need to practise playing the piano.

presently

This means 'soon', not 'at present'.

principal/principle

'Principal' is a noun or adjective that means 'main' or 'chief', eg the principal point; the principal of the college. 'Principle' is a noun that means 'fundamental characteristic, belief or doctrine', eg the principle of free speech.

supersede

Spelt with an 's' not a 'c'.

that/which

In general, use 'that' to define and 'which' to explain or inform:

- ❏ The report that was published last year was excellent.

Here, 'that' defines the report we're talking about, ie the one that was published last year, not the one that was published the year before.

- ❏ The report, which was published last year, has been accepted.

Here, 'which' introduces information not central to the meaning of the sentence: we could remove the middle section and it would still make sense, just as we could if it were in brackets.

So 'which' qualifies and usually follows a comma.

while/whilst

Use 'while'.

Index

Page numbers in bold
show where the subject
is explored in more depth.

Last,
but not
least,
avoid
clichés
like the
plague.

William Safire

[Emphasis] knows how to teach people to write well. But what really impressed us was the time and effort spent tailoring that to the M&S brand.

Jo Rook, Marks & Spencer

Probably the most practically useful course I've attended in recent years.

Tracy Gordon, Deloitte

Emphasis is one of the most professional organisations I have ever worked with.

Gerry Doyle, Gillette